KENTUCKY

Courtesy of

LINCOLN & ALLEN
B I N D E R Y

(503) 223-2035
1-800-824-1632
FAX (503) 223-1410

3033 N.W. YEON AVE.,
P.O. BOX 10745
PORTLAND, OREGON 97210

KENTUCKY

PHOTOGRAPHY BY JAMES ARCHAMBEAULT

TEXT BY THOMAS D. CLARK

GRAPHIC ARTS CENTER PUBLISHING COMPANY

PORTLAND, OREGON

International Standard Book Number 0-912856-74-2
Library of Congress Catalog Card Number 81-86037
Copyright © 1982 by Graphic Arts Center Publishing Company
P.O. Box 10306 • Portland, Oregon 97210 • 503/224-7777
Designer • Robert Reynolds
Typesetter • Paul O. Giesey/Adcrafters
Printer • Graphic Arts Center
Bindery • Lincoln & Allen
Printed in the United States of America

Page ii: The panorama of horses and spectators at the Keeneland Race Course near Lexington exemplifies the sport's pageantry and excitement.

Page 5: One hundred and thirteen-foot Yahoo Falls in McCreary County veils a rock shelter where some of Kentucky's pre-historic inhabitants once lived.

Above: Fall splendor of Kentucky Ridge State Forest along the Commonwealth's eastern border in Bell County. *Left:* From a perspective atop the peaks of Kingdom Come State Park, Appalachian ridges roll eastward in rhythmic topographical grandeur across Harlan and Letcher counties. *Overleaf:* Butterfly amid a full burst of iron-weed bloom in Morgan County.

The Wet Prong of Buffalo Creek, flowing atop the Mammoth Cave area into the Green River, traverses a part of the thousands of acres which comprise the federal reservation. The national park and cave are visited by thousands every year.

Above: Along a Boone County road, against the fading light of a summer day, a lone Kentucky farmhouse stands boldly outlined. *Overleaf:* Regular rows of tender young burley tobacco weave an intriguing agricultural pattern around a fertile Clinton County knoll.

Above: On the Rough River in Ohio County, a sugar maple spreads brilliant fall foliage inside a dome of azure. *Right:* Native Kentucky fescue in rich winter garb near Wolf Creek in Meade County. *Overleaf:* May-apple and blue-eyed Marys herald spring in the John James Audubon State Park, Henderson.

14

KENTUCKY

In the beginning of Anglo-American settlement, the hills of Kentucky were covered by dark, almost impenetrable forest, filled with laurel, rhododendron, and scores of other shrubs and flowering plants. This highland Eden, whose knobby western escarpment tilts down to the bluegrass plain, produced one of the widest varieties of trees and plants on the globe. One can only imagine now the magnificent American chestnuts which stood as sentinels on the horizon, Appalachian monarchs who were first to hail the sun and last to see it drop below the western rim. But the chestnuts competed equally with massive oaks, yellow or tulip poplars, black walnuts, butternuts, basswood, hickories, hard maples, and nearly a hundred other species.

Beneath this sheltering canopy, grazing animals trampled out paths between Cumberland Gap and the Falls of the Ohio. So efficiently did these engineers of nature choose their routes that they outlined many roads still in the modern Kentucky highway system. The buffalo especially had an innate sense for following the least taxing elevations and locating the safest fording places.

The first Anglo-Americans to enter the western Eden were long hunters who wandered far and wide from their Virginia and Carolina backcountry settlements, or from western Pennsylvania and Maryland. Wherever skins and furs could be found, they were there to take them. They learned the location of the important salt licks, the courses of streams, and the lay of the land. Some of these hunter-traders lugged packs of English-made goods — baubles, scalping knives, vermilion, tomahawks, cheap-john guns, and brilliantly colored textiles.

Kentucky is a mother pioneer western state, the first carved from the trans-appalachian wilderness. The sprawling country inside Cumberland Gap became the scene of fresh beginnings, and the thrust toward the greater American West. It was in Kentucky that the first band of American pioneer heroes had their seasoning and established claims to enduring fame. It was here, also, that a second generation of settlers met the challenges of the wilderness.

King of the crowd was that overshadowing figure, Daniel Boone. Well before he came to his earthly end in Missouri in 1820, Boone had shucked his sweaty hunter's garb and donned the legendary buckskins of books and poems. In 1775 a young Virginian traveling with Boone's trailblazing party recorded a description of the land which rolled out before them one morning. After fighting their way through mountain brush, across cane-lined streams and heartless ridges, the party stood at last atop a knobby hill, and, like the Children of Israel in Exodus, gazed over into the promised land. Before them, wrote Felix Walker, "A new and strange earth seemed to be presented to our view. So rich a soil we had never seen before; covered with clover in full bloom, the woods were abounding with wild game...It appeared that nature, in the profusion of her bounty, had spread a feast for all that lives."

Like all Edens, that which burst into view before young Walker had its serpents. It was at once the prized hunting ground and disputed border land between warring northern and southern Indians, both jealous of their claims. In that late March morning in 1775, Daniel Boone could point out to his companions many of the important landmarks he had learned in two years of wandering and hunting. He knew, perhaps better than anyone, the stream courses, the Indian trails, the location of the best lands, and the suddenness with which tragedy and death could overtake the unwary. Boone was born with a genius for managing Indian diplomacy. Otherwise, he could never have survived.

Others shared Boone and Walker's enthusiasm for the rolling lands of the Bluegrass. The year Boone's party arrived, George Rogers Clark came to Harrodsburg and quickly wrote his Tidewater, Virginia father, "A richer and more beautiful country than this I believe has never been seen in America yet." His extravagant praise was confirmed by other emigrants and visitors. The sophisticated Englishman Gilbert Imlay wrote back to a friend that all a settler had to do was girdle the trees and cut back the cane and he was ready to begin farming. In one season he could fill cribs and graneries with products of the fields, and crocks and bins with fruits of the orchard and vineyard.

Well before Imlay saw the Bluegrass in the spring of 1791, the roads and rivers leading into Kentucky were flush with settlers seeking security and fortune. Beaming in their eager, inquiring eyes was the dream of owning rich lands, of creating manorial estates equal to those in the Cottswolds, Kent, Sussex, Devon, and along the tidal rivers of Old Virginia.

Geographically, Kentucky is a state of expansive width and narrow girth, reaching from densely befogged Black Mountain against the eastern wall to the low-lying river bottoms of the Mississippi. Old-time Kentucky politicians made grandiloquent oratorical sweeps of this great distance when they proclaimed their loyalties to every Kentuckian living between "the Breaks of

Sandy in the Pine Mountain Range to Mills Point on the Mississippi." But within the arbitrary political boundaries designated by Virginia assemblymen in 1789, three or four separate and harmonious sections could have been carved.

Early in the first half of the eighteenth century, a French cartographer had drawn heavily on his imagination and in a Parisian dream represented the country as one covered in equal proportions with trees, buffaloes, and mounted Indian hunters. He was largely right on the first score, and partially so on the other two. Kentucky was a natural western "island" sealed in by the great rock wall on the east and the rivers on the north and west. And it was a game hunter's paradise. But the hunter could only enter it by narrow, rock-lined gaps and rivers, and once inside he faced resistance from man and nature.

The Ohio and Mississippi rivers sweep around most of Kentucky's northern and southwestern face and cut it off from the western part of the American continent. The Ohio, which meanders on an indecisive course, as if uncertain whether to cut southward and join the Mississippi, has historically been a "dare line" between North and South. Between Big Sandy and Mills Point is a sizable territory of sharp natural contrasts. A complex mountain range of peaks and rock-rimmed table lands lying above the shoulders of Appalachian ridges created a maze which trapped both fauna and man in a tight geographic enclosure of haze-shrouded hills and moist gorges and coves. Every pair of ridges spawned a hollow, and every hollow was split by a stream, often running fresh and pure from mountain springs.

Beginning on the slopes of Black Mountain in far eastern Kentucky, the Cumberland River slashes its valley out of unrelenting rock to wind a serpentine course through the heartland and sprawl lazily in a wide sweeping bend around Nashville, Tennessee. Pouring in a wild cataclysmic roar over the steep ledge near Williamsburg, Kentucky, it sets aglow a moonbow which never ceases to interest visitors to the Cumberland Falls Park. Cumberland's white-water South Fork, a stream which has caused almost as much argument between environmentalists and developers as its bubbling waters have created navigational sensations, ploughs its determined way out of the Tennessee hills. Once the Cumberland has bored through more than a hundred miles of ancient geology, it flattens out and heads northwestward out of Tennessee to pick up another thread of its Kentucky story. At its mouth it is little more than a lazy mill-pond held back by the Barkley Dam.

The Cumberland waters were the first west of Cumberland Gap to be reached by the famous long hunters. In fact, the trailbreaking Walker expedition of 1750 undertook to establish a permanent camp on the river's bank, but gave up in frustration. More persistent woodsmen wandered downstream to the great salt lick on the site of present-day Nashville, and in the course of time settlers moved along the Cumberland's course to establish a string of backwoods settlements.

Some of the late eighteenth century emigrants reached the new lands only to become hewers of wood and drawers of water, but foresighted ones among them established hefty claims along the prongs of the Elkhorn, the Stoner, Wolfe Run, Greer's Creek, and Town Branch, and along many another shallow-bed, limestone run. In miraculously short time they opened farms and built a succession of houses which reached Georgian and Greek Revival opulence. Here in the Bluegrass, they built the county towns of Lexington, Paris, Georgetown, Nicholasville, Richmond, Winchester, and Cynthiana. They stocked lush pastures with high-strung, thoroughbred sporting horses, finely bred sheep, imported cattle, and purebred hogs. They also cut hams that competed with those cured and smoked in Virginia.

The Bluegrass garnered the first settlers, and perhaps more than its part of the state's history, but dipping south and southwestward toward the confluence of the great rivers and a junction with the state of Tennessee lay another wilderness empire which was largely unexplored in 1775, when settlers arrived at Boonesboro and Harrodsburg. The broad Pennyrile (Pennyroyal) is a section where nature has been as lavish with trees and plants as its name implies. The startling exception, its western barrens, whose origins are still inadequately explained by botanists and geologists, is devoid of trees. Within the Pennyrile are found those other geological wonders, the Green River country caves. Though the Bluegrass has symbolized farming and livestock breeding in Kentucky, the broad and fertile Pennyrile fields fatten the state's agricultural statistical tables. The region has never boasted famous race horses or fancy imported cattle and sheep, but it has produced a substantial agrarian society. Its culture remains solidly land-based and strongly reminiscent of the Piedmont areas of Virginia and Carolina, with a strong essence of the Old Cotton South.

Kentucky forests and fields hospitably welcome nearly every

In a Dixiana Horse Farm paddock in Fayette County, a thoroughbred stallion cavorts in snow, freshly fallen.

species of birds known in the eastern United States, except those which only inhabit the coast. Twice a year the land is alive with the chirping, calls, and honkings of migrating flocks moving to and from nesting grounds. Many of these have come home to Kentucky to fatten on the largesse of the green land. In early spring, almost at the moment the "sarvice berry" bushes bloom, the first choruses of birdsong open, followed in May by a crescendo of joy and territorial proclamations. Resting and feeding grounds on the middle fly-way of waterbirds, Kentucky lakes and rivers host tremendous flocks of ducks, geese, and swans drifting south in fall, just ahead of freezing weather, and north in spring on the heels of thawing waters. In the dead of winter Kentucky is left largely a silent land. When the forests stand gaunt and bare, only a few feathered tenants break the silence. The pileated woodpecker, who tends his wooded domain in looping flights, uttering raucous screams, reminds us that not all nature is dormant.

In its early decades Kentucky was not only a mecca to western land hunters, but to botanists, ornithologists, and naturalists as well, including the father and son, F. A. and Andre Michaux, the eccentric Constantine Rafinesque, Alexander Wilson, and John James Audubon. Rafinesque spent eight stormy years rambling through Kentucky woods and fields in search of minerals and animal specimens and described his findings in a prodigious number of books and articles. Earlier, the dour Scotsman Alexander Wilson paddled his arduous way down the Ohio in a skiff. In search of bird specimens and subscribers to his *American Ornithologist,* he found in Louisville, Lexington, and Frankfort many interesting human specimens. His famous nine-volume work describes the birds. His travel notes open a fascinating window on early nineteenth century Kentucky society.

It was, however, the ubiquitous John James Audubon who captured the imagination of Kentuckians. Audubon ran a mill and store at the Falls of the Ohio, then downstream at Henderson. During his Kentucky sojourn, the famous painter and ornithologist met many of the early pioneers, including Daniel Boone. Audubon's *Delineations of American Scenery and Character* held a mirror to his former neighbors that was sometimes less than pleasing, but the natives never forgot him and named a state park, a museum, streets, and other landmarks in his memory.

In an almost startling historical paradox, central Bluegrass had largely outgrown its frontier background before the beginning of the nineteenth century to become a prosperous settled island in a sea of forest and backwoods society. So remarkable was the mature culture of the Bluegrass that it dominated social, political, and economic forces in the founding of the new Kentucky Commonwealth, in expressing western views in the United States Congress, and in controlling affairs in the Kentucky General Assembly.

The Bluegrass was a major way-station for touring eighteenth and nineteenth century foreign travelers who came to see how American democracy fared, to locate cheap land for settler groups, and to find scientific specimens. Many of the visitors lifted critical eyebrows at the restless human specimens who bolted their food, slept four and five abed in backwoods taverns, chewed tobacco, and boasted of the future promise of the country.

A fair majority of these Englishmen and Europeans traveled westward by the Ohio. If they came downstream from the north, they short-cut the great river loop and traveled overland from Maysville by way of Paris to Lexington, Frankfort, and Louisville. Reversing this route, those who came upstream from New Orleans departed by way of Maysville. In their published accounts, they wrote of people, land, politics, customs, and future prospects. Collectively, their books spread as much misinformation as fact. Among this transient horde came notables like General Lafayette, author Charles Dickens, and singer Jenny Lind, who was rushed off by P.T. Barnum to warble in Mammoth Cave's great central cavern. For these visitors, the rest of Kentucky might as well have been undiscovered. Few of them knew Appalachia existed.

The central area they saw and described sustained a rising agrarian aristocracy which tenaciously nurtured an English country gentleman's sense of living. Long before France and Spain relinquished their hold on the lower Mississippi, Kentucky flatboatmen drifted on month-long voyages southward to New Orleans aboard vessels loaded with meal, flour, bourbon whiskey, bales of hempen rope and coarse slave cloth, fruit brandy, and cured meats. These rowdy up-river men fetched home sacks of silver coins, shipped fancy goods by way of Philadelphia, ladened family coffers, and built Virginia-style Georgian homes constructed from lumber and brick "cut and burnt on the place." So important was the flatboat trade that central Kentuckians and their congressional representatives exerted unrelenting pressure on Thomas Jefferson's Administration to purchase the Louisiana Territory from France and were prepared to battle with Spain when

Kentucky's harvest of grain heads to a worldwide market from the broad farms of Fulton County.

The intricate pattern of Mammoth Cave's Drapery Room is the handiwork of millions of years of mineral-saturated waters.

that country seemed reluctant to relinquish its gulf coast empire.

Kentucky's economic future was shuffled in 1811 when Captain Nicholas Roosevelt anchored his clumsy steamer the *New Orleans* in Louisville. This event gave the Commonwealth a greater shaking than did the famous New Madrid Earthquake which occurred later that year, for steamboats hauled Kentucky produce downstream with even greater facility than flatboats and brought back a horde of money that enriched Bluegrass farmers. Evidence of the new prosperity was soon visible in rising homesteads and in towns like Lexington which, tucked away in the Kentucky heartland, was viewed as the "Athens of the West."

Growing in wealth and cultural sensitivity, many Kentuckians became almost militantly aware of the currents of conflict disturbing the Old World. In 1821, local newspaper columns were filled with news of the Greek revolutionary struggle against the heathen Turks, and Lexingtonians formed clubs and societies to support the cause of the cultural motherland. When Gideon Shryock returned home from Philadelphia after an apprenticeship with William Strickland, he designed a stately Greek Revival temple for the new statehouse. To erect his neo-classical symbol of democracy, Shryock used the handsome limestone of the Kentucky River's Tyrone bed. In time, Shryock designed other classical public buildings and made the private home with columns a status symbol.

Kentuckians, like many southerners, gave free rein to their romantic impulses. Reading Sir Walter Scott's Waverly novels in the affluent antebellum age, they imagined themselves knights and ladies ensconced behind feudal walls. Some raised spiny cottages with lavishly adorned pointed gables. Others copied the "big houses" of Scotland and England with their crenolated roof lines, pointed spires, cathedralesque windows, and heavy oaken doors. Along the Ohio River, Spanish and Caribbean architectural influences floated upstream aboard steamboats, and "New Orleans" houses lined the streets of Owensboro, Louisville, Henderson, and Maysville. Further upstream, Germans brought another concept of architecture — picturesque urban rowhouses standing flush with sidewalks and opening on rear private gardens.

Kentuckians brought some organized religion across the mountains with them, and a rousing seige of revivals at the opening of the nineteenth century gave that religion a distinctive, frontier dimension. In storms of emotionalism, groups splintered off into various sectarian bodies, including Mother Ann Lee's celibate Shaker community. All across Kentucky, congregations raised church houses as humble places of worship. In the towns, once things settled down, denominations raised pointed steeples to break the rural horizon. It was and still is the simple, white church house planted in a secluded nook of trees that characterizes both Kentucky religious devotion and architectural simplicity. The Shilohs, Enons, Mount Zions, and Mount Nebos lend a quiet charm to the countryside as symbols of a God-fearing people.

While architects designed stately public buildings and elegant porticoed homes, and carpenters and builders raised simple frame churches, a rising and prosperous landed aristocracy built elaborate double-parlors in their houses and filled them with family portraits painted by early nineteenth century artists. Matthew Harris Jouett may not enjoy the universal fame of the Wests, Sullys, Peales, and other American greats, but he enjoyed the high esteem of his subjects. He was Kentucky's own to be honored and cherished for all time to come. There were others — Joseph H. Bush, Oliver Frazier, John Grimes, and Samuel Woodson Price, who, like Jouett created a considerable gallery of Kentucky personages in the "Golden Age" of agrarian splendor.

Proud livestock breeders also employed artists to paint portraits of their prize animals. Swiss-born Edward Troye, of French parentage, early became an important animal painter. His portraits of Kentucky race horses and trotters include such immortals as Lexington, Glencoe, Maude S., American Eclipse, and Kentucky, who hang alongside portraits of grandfathers and grandmothers. Meanwhile, sculptors Joel Tanner Hart of Clark County and Frank Duveneck of Covington chiseled busts and statues of the famous and affluent. But the Kentucky artist who came closest to portraying the Commonwealth's natural beauty was Paul Sawyier of Madison County and Frankfort. Sawyier was a watercolorist and painter with a strong grounding in the style of the famous Hudson River School, and he captured the simple beauty of secluded nooks and corners of the Kentucky River Valley.

Editors of farm journals, who flocked to Kentucky to inspect the herds and flocks of such farms as Woodburn, Locust Hill, and Auvergne, by-passed the outlying subsistence farms. Outsiders reading their stories might have believed Kentucky was one grand pasture and all its social life revolved around fairs and livestock rings. Not so. Kentucky's rural dirt-farm population lived comfortably without assistance from farm editors and sporting magazines.

And they retained many of the old ways. They moved from pole cabins to double-log houses to the comfortable white cottages and tall two-story family seats which today stand as quiet and dignified landmarks to an important way of life. The century-old trees which surround their homes are, in their own way, an artistic heritage. Here, Kentucky's population made cultural contributions in the form of yeoman country life, preserving the folk music which it brought over the mountains as well as old dance forms, party games, and sports depending on personal prowess.

The loose geographical and sociological designation "Appalachia" has become almost a cult one. A third of the state has geographical and environmental attachments to this cohesive region, but more than that Appalachia is a state of mind. Like flood waters emptying into a darkening slough of eighteenth and early nineteenth century isolation, the early Appalachian population clamored through the eastern gaps in Pine Mountain, or drifted down the Ohio and up mountain stream laterals to settle away from the changing patterns of a rising American civilization.

Here, frontiersmen became mountaineers who clung tenaciously to the fixed social habits of their origins and generated their own traditions. Highlanders sang Old World ballads, spoke a quaint, seventeenth century English, believed stoutly in ancient superstitions, and were suspicious of "outside" influences. They also created their own original traditions and speech patterns. They looked to the abundant fauna and flora for foods, sport, and building materials. Shrubs and wild flowers which bloomed gloriously in the spring and bore fruit in the autumn offered a specific for man's ills. And the hills still hold men and women who are veritable folk pharmacopoeias of natural herbs and their powers.

Ties of kinship, patriarchial reverence, and emotional attachment to the land run strong. In a network of creeks, vales, and coves there has grown over two centuries a blood pattern of human relations. So intricate are highland relationships that many a man has settled his confusion by claiming kin to everyone in his neighborhood. A candidate for public office can often predict success by the number of his kinsmen in a precinct.

Like the rest of Kentucky, the Appalachian region is a land of sharp contrasts. Subsistence farmers maul a living out of thin soils, coal miners with blackened faces and lungs dredge the bowels of the hills for "black gold," while thousands of others have become the children of modern American industrialization. While some old customs have changed, others die slow deaths in the mountain corn patches and along the spring branches. The age-old mountain tradition of making moonshine whisky remains. There are enough stills hidden in the hills to keep revenue officers alert, although repeal of the Eighteenth Amendment, in the words of the wildcatter, "pret nigh ruint" the honest home distiller.

No aspect of Kentucky economic history is more heavily shrouded in the mist of legend than the origin of bourbon whisky. Who introduced the process of turning clear liquid into an amber-colored one? How did he discover the use of charred barrels, and what effect did limestone water have on quality? The old story that the preacher Lewis Craig was first to distill bourbon whisky at his Scott County mill may be seriously questioned by more recent and dependable research. In November 1823, the *Kentucke Gazette* published a recipe for making sweet mash whisky which emphasized the usefulness of the human hand as a temperature gauge for the painfully hot brew of water, mash, meal, and yeast. Until 1804, whisky making was largely a domestic enterprise, but by the end of the Civil War it had become a major commercial industry. Between 1865 and 1918, millions of gallons of the amber fluid were shipped from warehouses in Lexington, Lawrenceburg, Bardstown, New Haven, Louisville, and Owensboro. The names of Kentucky's famous distillers competed with those of politicians for national fame. Brand names were as appealing as romantic Kentuckians could make them, and the adjective "old" was almost as indispensable as the mash formula itself. At one time, bourbon whisky was made by using bluegrass water, and the limestone tradition lives on as a legend of the trade, as does the illusion that the business operates at the head of a hollow where, drop by drop, the liquor drips from the still under the eagle eye of an octogenarian gauger.

Kentuckians are ambivalent about their liquid resources. Of the state's 120 counties, more than ninety are "dry." In some instances, the drouth has settled upon individual towns and portions of counties, and there may be some truth in the oft-quoted accusation that ministers and bootleggers join hands to keep their territories free of bars and liquor stores.

On big special occasions, like Derby Day, Kentuckians like to dream of the time mint juleps were a more common beverage than spring water. Every real goatee-stroking colonel had to justify his rank by harboring a lush spring branch bed of mint, a sideboard

What was once the backbone of Kentucky's public elementary school system is exemplified by this solitary one-room schoolhouse on Daniels Creek in southeastern Kentucky.

groaning under the weight of sterling silver julep cups, a plentiful stock of sugar and ice, and a butler plying guests with frosty sweetness and spirituous cheer. Only the prized julep cups have really survived as the expert julep concocters passed on to serve more celestial sideboards. An imitation of the dream of drinks J. Soule Smith described so eloquently is now served every first Saturday in May. Governors, Derby hosts, and the Honorable Order of Kentucky Colonels salvage part of the tradition by serving country ham washed down with bourbon. Old Taylor, Old Fitzgerald, Jim Beam, Ancient Age, Old Glenmore, Maker's Mark, and many other brands still hold their own against alien brews.

Two broad walls of the new library and archives in Frankfort hold the works of Kentucky authors. Collectively, they have created a literature which passes under the broad generic title of "Kentuckiana." In the formative years of the roaring forties when men and women were intent on establishing a mature society, less than a half dozen fiction writers undertook to capture the Kentucky spirit in their writings. In post-Civil War decades, there was a growing realization that many of the old patterns of Kentucky life were being swept away by the raw materialistic age. For some there was a nostalgic grasping at the past before it faded.

In a series of seminal books and articles, James Lane Allen savored the life of bluegrass neighbors, examined their prejudices, and exhibited a profound sensitivity to agrarian life in a changing era. While Allen wrote of the settled and sophisticated ways of the Bluegrass, life in Appalachia was troubled to the breaking point by an outbreak of senseless family feuds. Men warred on their neighbors over boundaries, women, pigs, moonshine stills, Civil War angers, and personal slights, some so vague no one could precisely recall them. Hatfields stalked McCoys along the Tug Fork of Big Sandy, Bakers drew deadly beads on Whites in the wilds of Clay County, the French clan shot at Eversoles, and Hargisses and Callahans mowed down Marcums and Cockrills with the same abandon they shot squirrels out of scalybark trees in the Breathitt hills. While they riddled Kentucky's image, few dared speak their minds in defense of civil decency.

John Fox, Jr. of Bourbon County in the Bluegrass was intrigued by the sharp contrast between life in his native region and the hills. Going to live in the highlands, he wrote numerous stories and novels, fixing in the *Heart of the Hills* and *Hell fer Sartain* a historical moment in Kentucky civilization which never again will

be repeated. It was Chad Buford, however, who helped draw the clearest line between these two segments of Kentucky civilization. He endured the traumatic ordeal of deciding whether to ride away amidst a wild flurry of rebel yells with bluegrass kinsmen and fight with Morgan's Confederate volunteers or to return to his people in the hills and give support to the nation. Allen and Fox, Kentucky's literary progenitors, spawned a healthy brood of descendants.

No literary Kentuckian has scaled greater heights than Robert Penn Warren, born in 1905, in Guthrie. In more than thirty books he has turned to his homeland for substance and inspiration. In his early novel *Night Rider,* he caught rural Kentucky in a moment when its civilization rested on dead center. In his epic poem *Brothers to Dragon,* the nationally acclaimed poet sounded the depths of Jeffersonian traditions and the behavior of paranoic slaveowners. In *World Enough and Time,* he directed the novelist's penetrating beam on the Beauchamp-Sharpe Tragedy of the 1820s, a gripping drama of inflamed politics and cold-blooded murder which included a public hanging, a suicide, a lover's pact, and the burial of Jeroboam Beauchamp and Anne Cooke in a common grave. Warren's *Jefferson Davis Regains His Citizenship* focuses the memories of a rural Kentucky boyhood, while hundreds of his poems investigate the meaning of life.

In the ridge country of the upper reaches of the Ohio, Jesse Stuart of Greenup County has surpassed all other Kentucky authors in sheer volume. At once poet, short-story writer, novelist, and sharp, non-fiction commentator, his people eke out simple lives, snatching a meager subsistence from their coves, never seeing themselves as deprived of life's bounties, or building bright hopes for the future. Elizabeth Madox Roberts of Springfield mined another vein of knob-country rurality. Her involved romantic symbolism in *Black is My True Love's Hair* expresses the seasons and life of people and land. The quiet but masterful James Still of Hindman has caught another rhythm of Appalachian life in *River of Earth, On Troublesome,* and *Run for the Albertas.* Still's regional dialect is so accurate it suggests the music of a well-tuned violin. Like Stuart he is an eloquent chronicler of his land, understanding its rugged harshness and the compromises his humble neighbors have made to survive.

Among local genera writers, Harriett Arnow has written of the soul-blighting experiences of thousands of Kentucky country people who were torn away from their ancient folk moorings

Changing shifts: Pike County underground miners before the mouth of a heavily producing coal mine in Kentucky's rich eastern field.

because they were unable to sustain themselves on land which, in the 1930s, was rapidly subdivided and dredged of its substance. In *Mountain Path, Hunter's Horn,* and *The Doll Maker* she described how hill-country Kentuckians attempted to keep their basic values as they adapted to new and indifferent surroundings. Meanwhile, on the lower Kentucky River, Wendell Berry has, since the 1960s, made eloquent response to the inner surgings of the land in his poems, and in *Nathan Coulter* and *The Memory of Old Jack.* Berry is a persuasive apostle of natural men living off the bounties of cared-for land. His characters are attuned to the rhythm of the seasons, to the breedings and birthings of domestic animals, and to the castings and harvestings of crops. They accept with grace whatever the seasons bring to the lower Kentucky river valley.

At the end of the Great Depression and on the eve of World War II, when coal would again be in demand, John F. Day, a skilled newspaper reporter, drove and walked through eastern Kentucky. This land, which had fallen under the impress of greedy industrialization, was one of unemployed miners, moonshiners, tawdry honky-tonks, snake-waving religious sects, and wholesale cultural blight. There is pathos, even humor, in the rich folk tapestry unrolled in Day's *Bloody Ground,* a landmark in Appalachia's documentary literature. Harry Caudill of Whitesburg takes up the story of eastern Kentucky where Fox and Day left off. His *Night Comes to the Cumberland* sounded a clear call for a vigorous reevaluation of Kentucky mountain culture and its headlong rush into the modern world.

From the moment John Filson gave creative editorial assistance to Daniel Boone in recording his "autobiography" there has sprung into existence a flourishing crop of historians, biographers, poets, novelists, and essayists. But no single author has proved capable of bringing the stretch of Kentucky's historical and physical being into a single novel. Intangible forces in the lives of men and regions have obstinately worked against a common portrayal.

Kentucky's most consistent writers over the long haul are its newspaper editors and reporters. In mid-summer, 1787, John Bradford began a stout tradition when he pulled the first issue of *Kentucke Gazette's* ink-smeared four sheets from the press in Lexington. An all-consuming interest in politics has fertilized a strong state press. At Frankfort, the state capital, competing editors ran columns on national and state politics, advertised the services of stud horses, described run-away slaves, announced the arrival of new shipments, spun humorous yarns, lambasted their political enemies, and wrote glowing recommendations to St. Peter upon the departure of local subscribers. And every four years Kentucky editors raised a mighty shout of favoritism in support of gubernatorial and presidential candidates.

Editors had the gall of billy goats, were expert rifle shots, drank an unconscionable amount of bourbon whisky, and spoke ex-cathedra on all subjects. In 1831 a brash young Yankee who flung fire from his fingertips pitched feet foremost into the Kentucky editorial community. George Dennison Prentice of the *Louisville Daily Journal* became one of the most frequently quoted editors in America. Prentice went into presidential campaigns head down, roaring damnation to the opposition. At Frankfort, the highly capable Albert Gallatin Hodges kept an eagle eye on the deeds and misdeeds of governors and legislators and devoted generous space to the publication of humorous frontier stories.

In grim times, thoughtful editors turned their energies toward keeping Kentucky neutral in the Civil War and undoubtedly helped to prevent the Commonwealth from rashly seceding. By war's end, however, the old editors had grown too feeble and weary to combat the excesses of radical Reconstruction. In Louisville, the *Courier, Democrat,* and *Journal* merged in the *Louisville Courier-Journal* with young "Marse" Henry Watterson of Tennessee as editor. For half a century "Marse Henry," who wrote and spoke with the eloquence of Henry Clay, was the clearest editorial voice in the New South, a voice heard at the crossroads and in the United States Capitol. The *Courier-Journal* remains both a sophisticated, national-international urban paper and a local, folksy, social and political beacon.

Out on the front line of western expansion, Kentucky was forced to be a militant island of American civilization. Every border conflict threatened its existence, and, in a sense, every Kentucky pioneer who endured the hardships of fighting back the British and Indians and building a log cabin was a hero. Those who actually campaigned along the border against heavy odds won lasting glory. The roll of Kentucky men and women who stood resolutely against border attackers is long and revered. Deeply inscribed in memory are the names of those outnumbered stalwarts who fought back the enemy at Boonesboro, Bryan's Station, Logan's Fort, and Fort McClellan, among them Daniel Boone, Simon Kenton, Benjamin Logan, Richard Calloway, James Harrod, and Gabriel Jones.

An annual rite: the blessing of the Iroquois Hunt Club Hounds at Grimes Mill, Fayette County.

George Rogers Clark stands above the crowd because he invaded the enemy's home territory and won.

Through force and circumstance the military tradition was firmly planted in Kentucky soil. In time, almost every village street was trampled by greenhorn militiamen who gathered on muster days to march, drink, and frolic in preparation for campaigns north of the Ohio. The rank of captain, major, colonel, or general carried with it a mark of lifetime respect and prestige. Isaac Shelby, Kentucky's first governor, came into office with a tiny cadre of aides bearing military titles, and the General Assembly concerned itself with military matters in almost every session.

The War of 1812 was one of Kentucky's finest hours. Its militiamen confronted British and Indians on the Wabash, at Frenchtown, and in Canada at the River Thames. Toward the end, doughty old Governor Shelby, a celebrated Revolutionary War hero, marched at the head of troops. The battle names Tippecanoe, Raisin, Frenchtown, Put-in-Bay, Thames, and New Orleans became sacrosanct, and Kentuckians named their rapidly multiplying counties, towns, and villages for battles and heroes.

It was the Civil War, however, which sorely tested Kentucky's military mettle. Only two other states in the Union were as torn by divided sentiments and loyalties. A border slave state in which only a relatively small part of the population owned slaves, Kentucky feared military invasion. Overwhelmingly, Kentuckians were dedicated to the sanctity of constitutional government, a feeling strengthened by the services of famous sons like Breckinridge, Clay, Johnson, and Crittenden. More significantly, the migration of its native population had established blood ties with the West and South. And equally binding, it had strong commercial interests in all sections. Clearly, Kentucky had little to gain and much to lose in a civil war. Consequently, the Commonwealth struggled mightily to reconcile North and South, then to establish the state's neutrality, a condition which was flagrantly violated.

For Kentucky the Civil War was a tragic, personal conflict. It divided families, political parties, communities, and institutions. In the end, almost three times as many native sons served the Union cause, but the conflict produced a host of Union and Confederate heroes. Fortunately, Kentucky never became a major battleground, but in the War's closing years it bore the brunt of ferocious guerilla attacks which robbed and pillaged defenseless populations. For Kentucky, the Civil War would be a distinct political and economic dividing line. Never again would it claim the position of favor and influence it enjoyed in the prosperous years after 1830. Its frontier had vanished, and no blocks of unclaimed lands remained to attract new blood. Ex-Confederates miraculously gained control of the Kentucky political system, and not until the opening years of this century was the hold of the "brigadiers" broken.

In subsequent wars Kentuckians have given a good account of themselves. World War I, World War II, Korea, and Vietnam produced Medal of Honor heroes. Kentucky's contribution to American history has been great. It has been a mother state, and everywhere on the continent are cherished sons and daughters like Robert Penn Warren, David Wark Griffith, Loretta Lynn, Rosemary Clooney, Jean Ritchie, John F. Day, Cleanth Brooks, Muhammad Ali, and Harriett Arnow. In earlier years, Daniel Boone, Henry Clay, Kit Carson, Simon Kenton, Ninnian Edwards, Francis Preston Blair, and John Jordan Crittenden, along with a small army of territorial governors and judges, set their mark on the nation. No one knows how many plain people left the motherland to plod their way collectively into the history of western American civilization. Wherever a fresh frontier could be penetrated, Kentuckians were on hand to help bear the brunt of trailbreaking. Conditioned to withstand elements, animals, hostile Indians, and deprivation, they took seriously the heritage of Boone and Kenton. Every fresh land rush, south or west, drew Kentuckians away from their homes to seek fame and fortune. Much of the Anglo-American population of Missouri claimed Kentucky roots, as did the pioneers of Indiana and Illinois.

Of these emigrating families, two stamped their names imperishably on the pages of American history. The first, the poverty-ridden Lincolns, began their trek westward in Philadelphia and settled on the thin soil of Sinking Creek Farm in what is now LaRue County. Here, among the folds of the dividing Muldraugh Hills, they eked out a bare living. The land which they occupied still remains an open physical document of the frontier's mighty challenges. On a road beyond the crown of Muldraugh Hill stands the earliest house Abraham Lincoln clearly recalled. Eventually the Lincolns packed lock-stock-and-barrel and moved to Indiana Territory, then to Illinois, where Abe reached maturity.

Scarcely a hundred miles to the southwest lived the Davis family. Samuel and Jane Davis had left Georgia backcountry to settle in what is now Todd County. On their modest farm at Fairview their tenth child, Jefferson, was born. When the delta cotton lands of Mississippi were opened, the Davises moved downstream. In the course of history Abraham Lincoln and Jefferson Davis stood in opposition to each other, one as President of the United States, the other as President of the Confederacy. What if Abraham Lincoln's family had moved to the cotton lands, and the Davises had moved westward across the Indiana and Illinois backwoods?

Non-political sons and daughters have left the Commonwealth to achieve varying degrees of fame. Born the daughter of livestock trader George Moore and Mary Campbell Nation, hatchet-wielding crusader Carrie generated the fire of her Scotch-Irish ancestry. Her home, tucked away on a dim farm road atop the Dix River Cliff, is scarcely marked today. Ironically, Carrie warred against the liquid products her native people bragged about and consumed in drouth-quenching quantities. In an equally strong-willed vein, Sophinisba Breckinridge, daughter of one of Kentucky's most distinguished families, in an age when Kentucky women of her class remained home to be courted by socially acceptable young men, worked with Jane Addams in Hull House, and later became a pioneering professor in social work and sociology at the University of Chicago.

The strength of Kentuckians and their lives is recalled in the story of Jane Todd Crawford. In 1809, Dr. Ephraim McDowell, asked to attend Mrs. Crawford at the birth of twins, discovered she was not pregnant but carrying an enormous ovarian tumor, and pronounced the death sentence. Nevertheless, he agreed to operate without benefit of either anesthetic or antiseptic, and Mrs. Crawford accepted his offer. She rode horseback to Danville, and on Christmas day the doctor removed a twenty-pound mass from her abdomen. In a letter to a friend twenty years later, Dr. McDowell wrote: "The intestines, as soon as an opening was made, ran out upon the table and remained out about thirty minutes and, being Christmas day, they became so cold that I thought it proper to bathe them in tepid water previous to my replacing them; I then returned them and stitched up the wound and she was perfectly well in twenty-five days." Mrs. Crawford was made out of stern stuff. Two or three days after the operation, she got out of bed and swept her room. She was later to immigrate to Indiana, and to survive her physician by a decade or more.

Arthur Krock, a native of Glasgow, learned his trade on the Louisville Times and the Courier-Journal before he joined The New York World, and, later, The New York Times. With a remarkable ability to cultivate the friendship and confidence of politicians in the nation's capital and throughout the western world, Krock's columns were given serious reading, and his advice influenced public decisions. In another media, David Wark Griffith, son of a Confederate general, became a pioneer in the development of the moving picture industry. An inventor of new techniques, and director of a dozen films, he gained lasting fame as the director of The Birth of a Nation. Along with Henry Clay, Abraham Lincoln, Jefferson Davis, and Alben Barkley, Griffith is honored with a commemorative United States postage stamp.

These are some of the Kentucky men and women caught up in America's restless migrations. With them went thousands of sons and daughters, some clutching newly won university diplomas, to seek careers. They moved in droves, first to the virgin lands of the expanding West, and later to the cities. No one can estimate Henry Ford's impact on Kentucky alone. The age of the automobile carried Kentuckians to "Deetroit" and other northern industrial cities in restless waves. But the "O'Tucks" or "KY's" as many of them were called never made a clean break with home. For almost a half century roads running south from American industrial cities have swarmed with homesick natives "running down home to sop up a little of their raisin'."

A story-telling race, Kentuckians have found both whisky and politics popular topics of conversation. Since settlers first plodded over wilderness trails, they have analyzed the workings of politics and reminisced about the shenanigans of office-seekers now safely beneath the sod. For over two centuries, politics has lubricated democratic government and held Kentucky together. In earlier days, stump-speakings gathered crowds at militia musters, barbecues, burgoos, and courthouse debates. Prudent candidates stayed as far away from serious issues as their opponents would permit and stuck to repartee, bull-voiced oratory, and the praise of God, home, and motherhood.

Kentucky's political past is rich in stories of the great Shelby, Breckinridges, Clays, Carlisle, Goebel, and Stanley. Today one can sit in Gideon Shryock's tidily restored old statehouse and almost hear the echo of the volleyings of legislators of another age on subjects great and small. These rampant statesmen came down from the hills, up from the Purchase, out of Louisville and

A public forum in Mackville, Washington County on a winter day
when crops are cast, fish are caught, and politics damned.

Kentuckians' love of basketball begins at birth. Most family homes boast a basketball hoop for year-round shooting.

Lexington, from below the Green, and along the Cumberland to make laws, seek personal favors, and weigh such burning issues as the location of roads, the licensing of ferries, and sheep-killing dogs. Collectively, their actions lie entombed in hundreds of volumes of laws, legal codes, and court decisions.

These laws, however, have not impressed constituents as much as the characters who enacted them. Their stories, repeated, exaggerated, and glossed over, comprise a rich body of humor and color which Kentuckians cherish. It is a tradition which runs deep on the stump and in the newspapers. The *Courier-Journal's* master of commonplace Kentucky affairs was the shrewd political analyst Allan Trout, who led a double life as front-page reporter and back-page professor of barnyard science. When Trout had conducted his last crusade, distributed his last packet of gourd seeds, and whittled away the last piece of red cedar with his prized Barlow knife, he bequeathed his rural fiefdom to Joe Creason of Benton. Creason's column was more popular than *Journal* editorials and more humorous than a rip-snorting political campaign.

Kentucky's plush horse industry has also generated its share of anecdotes. It is sometimes difficult to sort out serious and whimsical matters in the history of breeding and racing horses. Behind every big auction or race are the stories of owners, breeders, trainers, and race track touts who sustain the sport. The horse enjoys a special niche in Kentucky, first for its heroic services in bearing settler and goods across the mountains, then as a source of power and energy. Historically, the first Kentucky horse race may have been run on the old Wilderness Road, when one emigrant challenged another to best his nag.

The first United States census revealed there were more horses than people in most Kentucky settlements. Almost before churches were organized there was a jockey club, and early legislators enacted laws prohibiting heedless jockeys from racing their mounts up and down muddy town streets. Tracks were organized early at Crab Orchard and Lexington, where the popular frontier quarter races were run, and advertisements for stallions appeared from the beginning in the *Kentucke Gazette*. These animals, imported from Virginia and England, were the foundation of Kentucky's blood horse tradition.

In 1875 Price McGrath's Aristides opened a new chapter in Kentucky horse racing history when he galloped home ahead of the pack to win the first Kentucky Derby at Churchill Downs. Since then, more than one hundred horses have glorified their owners on the first Saturday in May by winning the Derby. This event, which attracts world-wide attention, brings to Louisville an enormous throng of people, among them presidents, governors, senators, movie actors, and television personalities. It is an annual bonanza for Louisville hotels, merchants, and service people as over 100,000 spectators arrive to watch the first jewel in racing's Triple Crown. The day begins with the customary Derby breakfast. Discussions about trainers, jockeys, and the winner abound. But all speculation ends as the thoroughbreds complete the grueling mile-and-one-quarter race.

Four race tracks and the Red Mile Trotting Track in Lexington hold dual racing seasons, each gathering in crowds come partly to enjoy the pure aesthetics of noble horses in motion, partly to enjoy crowd excitement, largely to make hard cash investments. Off the race track, hotels, exclusive clubs and private homes bubble over with parties and commotion.

A more private world revolves around the horse sales held in Lexington. Here the aspiring and the rich, checkbook in hand, pay staggering prices for each new crop of yearlings, hoping to find another Secretariat or Nashua, to say nothing of a Man-O-War. Lexington becomes a focal center for much of the horse world, and the sales arenas take on the coloration of the frenzied grain pit in the Chicago commodities exchange.

The true beauty of the horse world, however, lies elsewhere. The rolling swales of bluegrass farms encased behind rock and white, oak-plank fences form a broad band of parkland. On the prongs of the Elkhorn, in Bourbon, Scott, Fayette, Woodford, Clark, and Jessamine counties, are the picture book farms like Calumet, Dixiana, Claiborne Farm, Hamburg, Almahurst, Spendthrift, Walnut Hall, Castleton, and Darby Dan. This green world is largely self-contained in both its human and business relationships. Its people speak a specialized horse vernacular, cherish their history, and, like their neighbors in the greater periphery of agrarian Kentucky, live by the seasons.

Aspects of the exploration and settlement of virgin Kentucky in some ways resembled a sporting event. The western woods were a hunter's paradise for both Indians and Anglo-American adventurers, and the state's early history is colored with stories of hunting. German craftsmen, who brought three centuries of gunmaking to a glorious climax in mid-eighteenth century Pennsylvania, called

As on Irish moors, central Kentucky limestone fences wander.
Pleasant Hill, Mercer County.

their rifles *Kentucky*. In decades to come these long-barreled instruments of destruction laid low squirrels, British, and Indians with equal vengeance. They roared at the Blue Licks, at Tippecanoe, the Thames, and at New Orleans. Or as Samuel Woodward wrote in "The Hunters of Kentucky," which sent the blood of local marksmen coursing:

But Jackson he was wide awake, and wasn't scared with trifles,
For well he knew what aim we take with our Kentucky rifles;
So he marched us down to 'Cypress Swamp'; the ground was
*   low and mucky.*
There stood 'John Bull', in martial pomp, but here was
*   old Kentucky.*

Appalachian highlanders embellished Kentucky's reputation for deadly marksmanship. Whether shooting squirrels or neighboring enemies, their unwavering aim excelled. Kentucky's woods, rivers, and lakes have ever attracted game, a fact which made possession of a gun as necessary as owning a good pocket knife. Earlier Kentuckians undertook to prove their individual superiority by shooting at targets for beef, outlifting their fellows at cabin raisings and log rollings, wrestling, and racing. They also indulged in less celebrated forms of spectator sports like gander pullings and bear baitings. With the exception of horse racing, it was not until after the Civil War that Kentucky sports were organized and played by formal rules.

Today, the sporting heart of Kentucky is unalterably committed to basketball. From the most modest elementary school to major universities, basketball seasons approach the erratic pixilations of dog days. When a Kentucky university coach recruits a top scorer, metropolitan newspapers crackle with excitement. Basketball hogs the loyalties of preachers, professors, attorneys, and crusty work-stained codgers huddling about country store stoves. Roman legions never marched so triumphantly, and trumpeters never winded the horn with the vigor of high school bandsmen. Led by cheerleaders and majorettes, mobs of fans rattle the rafters of gymnasiums. In their moments of glory, staid old towns change the names of time-honored streets to "Avenue of Champions."

So Kentucky's worlds revolve perpetually in concentric, Saturn-like circles, which, whirling around each other without merging, glory in the fact they are part of the Commonwealth. Physically, modern Kentucky is at once a land of breath-taking natural beauty and a testimonial to man's defilement. The haze-shrouded folds of hills which roll out from Pine Mountain are soul-lifting in majesty and space. This pastoral Kentucky, however, is rapidly being submerged by the invasion of industry, crowded shopping malls, urban sprawl, and a rapidly growing non-farm population. What was once a great wilderness eden is now laced together by million-dollar-a-mile highways which slash through rocky hillsides and thrust across rivers to collapse distances and erase sectional boundaries. A modern traveler can traverse Daniel Boone's two-year journey in less than two hours and not break the fifty-five-mile speed limit.

The longhunters, trailbreakers, and land scouts themselves planted the seeds of change. For two centuries their descendants nurtured those seeds. They have dammed up rivers to create vast lakes, gnawed their way through mountains to snatch up rich veins of coal, and strewn the countryside with the artifacts of modern civilization. Yet blessed islands of nature remain in the Daniel Boone National Forest, the national monuments about Cumberland Gap, Mammoth Cave, and the Lincoln Homestead, and in the wilderness peninsula between the Cumberland and Tennessee rivers. Not always astute in protecting its rich natural resources, Kentucky does preserve the sites of the Natural Bridge, Cumberland Falls, Carter Caves, Fairview, Lilly's Woods, and a half dozen other historic and natural areas. And Louisville distiller Isaac Bernheim dedicated his Muldraugh Hills knob land holdings as a magnificent public preserve.

If it were possible to stay the changes that the passage of time brings, most Kentuckians would choose to maintain the status quo. Self-assured prophets are certain that at the end of this century, Kentucky's foundation stone — the subsistence family farm, will be a museum piece; that the population will almost have doubled; that in place of man's traditional relationships with the land an urban society will claw furiously at the hills to create standing room. These prophets ignore the historic fact that after two centuries Kentucky still holds green breathing space.

Kentucky's rural traditions took shape in that time of leisurely seasoning, and there still thrives a vibrant group of obstinate and provincial humanity in the broad stretch of territory between Cumberland Gap and Reelfoot Lake who are ready if necessary to stand off a radical thrust of change, even the sudden burst of the revolutionary, twenty-first century.

EASTERN KENTUCKY

In a world of dramatically steep terrain, slashed by countless and often
unpredictable rivers and streams, the people cling tenaciously to a way of life
that mirrors the ruggedness and isolation of this beautiful land.

Above: Frequently described in the writings of Jesse Stuart, a modest, eastern
Kentucky farmstead sits amid pastures and fields near Elliottsville, Rowan
County. *Left:* Nature's surrender to fall: leaves and pine needles afloat on the
surface of a blackwater pond in the Red River Gorge.

Above: The famous 265-foot suspension, covered bridge at the village of Sherburne in Fleming County. Underneath its roof thousands of travelers once crossed the Licking River. *Right:* Rays of morning sun first sweep across Black Mountain, Kentucky's highest peak at 4,145 feet. Harlan County.

Above: Restored Hensley Settlement atop a Pine Mountain "flat" in Cumberland Gap National Historical Park. *Left:* A stand of hardwoods in Lilly Cornett Woods, Letcher County. The virgin trees are a monument to a dedicated home-grown conservationist who withstood the pressures of loggers and strip-miners.

The bare ribs of spiny Appalachia lie exposed in Bell County's Daniel Boone National Forest. The extreme ruggedness of cliff lines, benches, and coves have ever challenged human invaders.

Above: Appalachian spring. The eternal triumvirate of rural Kentucky: man, mules, and plow turning the land. *Overleaf:* Early morning fog hovering above Martin's Fork Lake in Harlan County veils a father and son bass fishing off a wooded point.

Atop Pine Mountain near Cumberland Gap, a primitive hand-riven paling fence
casts shadows across a snowy landscape in the Hensley Settlement.

Above: Conifers and boulders lie silently under a snowy mantle in Wolfe County's Tight Hollow. The Pottsville Escarpment forms a wide geological crescent around the Bluegrass. *Overleaf:* From Tator Knob, morning fog traces forest ridges in the Daniel Boone National Forest, Menifee County.

Above: A stately rural church stands sedately against a stark winter background along U.S. Highway 2 in Greenup County. *Right:* Laurel Lake on a soft summer morning thrusts a watery forefinger into an uppermost cove just off the famous Wilderness Trail. Laurel County.

Above: A crescent moon hovers above the Ashland Oil and Refining Company on the Big Sandy River at Catlettsburg. *Left:* A mountain waterfall, half-frozen under the pall of winter, plunges into its time-worn "blue hole." Jackson County.

A rare orchid drooping a pale bloom beneath a purple hood glorifies spring woods about Buckhorn Lake State Park, Perry County. This delicate beauty is a dramatic treasure among Kentucky's rich and varied collection of wild flowers.

This aging homestead in the foothills of Powell County has withstood many a storm as well as the wear-and-tear of generations to become a treasured Kentucky landmark. Many pioneer homesteads survive along the backroads.

Above: Atop a knoll near Pilot, Estill County, a generation of Kentuckians lie amid forest they once cleared from their land. *Right:* Along a country road in Knox County, hemlocks frame a stand of young tulip poplars at the height of fall.

Above: Rock Bridge Arch in the Red River Gorge has been eroded for millions of years by Swift Camp Creek, Wolfe County. *Left:* Near Cumberland Falls on the Cumberland River, Eagle Falls empties its flood over a steep limestone ledge. *Overleaf:* The Licking River in Fleming County, near Battle Run, flows placidly in a deep-shaded summer pool.

Gray's Arch, dramatically outlined at sunrise in the Red River Gorge, Daniel Boone National Forest. One of the most impressive geological arches in eastern Kentucky, it stands among approximately eighty other similar formations.

Above: A venerable, clapboard log cabin with its loft room, drooping porch, and sturdy chimney of hand-hewn stone defies time and elements near Vaughn's Mill, Powell County. *Overleaf:* Steep, forested hills dominate the shoreline of man-made Cave Run Lake, sun-drenched on a summer day. Rowan County.

Above: Wooden walkways flank Augusta's stately row of ante-bellum homes, lined up in review along the Ohio River. Bracken County. *Right:* Coal-laden cars await trans-shipment from Greenup County in the great assembly yard at Russell. The precious bituminous fuel heads to market from Appalachian mines.

Above: On the Ohio River, the steeples and cupolas of Maysville's skyline are graceful markers above the mouth of Limestone Creek, where floods of emigrants first touched the soil of their future homeland. *Left:* Lick Falls pours its crystal burden into the rock-lined basin of Grayson Lake, Carter County.

Near the top of Pine Mountain, stark hardwood trees locked in winter open a deep funnel through early morning fog. Pine Mountain State Park, Bell County.

A segment of the giant Armco Steel plant pokes its industrial head into a gusty winter storm on the Big Sandy River at Ashland. The lower reaches of this Ohio River lateral are intimately tied up with Kentucky's industrial development.

Above: Winter sun glances across the ridge from Chimney Rock in the Red River Gorge, Wolfe County. *Right:* A time when one could live forever. An early Kentucky autumn with its burst of deciduous, harvest-season colors from the top of the Auxier Ridge, Red River Gorge Geological Area.

Above: The fiercely determined Big Sandy slices a rocky course through the breathtaking "Breaks" in the hogback of the Pine Mountain Range. Pike County. *Left:* At the head of a deep forest cove in Menifee County, tulip poplars and a mixture of highland flora frame this ancient boulder. *Overleaf:* Shillalah Creek washes and pitches its white-crested course near Cumberland Gap.

A shaft of early morning sun thrusts through heavy foliage along Cave Branch in Carter Caves State Resort Park to burn away a veil of mist. Within this public preserve flourishes a wide variety of wild flowers and shrubs.

Above: A weather-beaten farmhouse in an isolated spot in northeastern Kentucky emerges from the uneven light of a rainy winter's day. *Overleaf:* Buried deep inside a primeval setting, the environmentally embattled Devil's Jump on the Big South Fork of the Cumberland races around rocky barriers.

Discovered by the first Anglo-American explorers, grandiloquent Cumberland Falls is set against a background of forest trees on the Cumberland River between McCreary and Whitley counties.

From Pine Mountain to the Mississippi River the wild dogwood heralds the coming of spring. Here this sweet harbinger accents a burgeoning woodland in Johnson County's Licking River Valley.

Cattle, viewed from the Woodford County side of the Kentucky River above the Oregon Landing, graze on the hills of a Mercer County farm. Raising cattle, a traditional Kentucky activity, is second to tobacco in yielding a cash income.

CENTRAL KENTUCKY

Hard-working, prosperous, yet decidedly easy-going, central Kentuckians
display an unrestrained and well-founded pride for this rare and tranquil heartland
of the Bluegrass State that boasts horse farms, bourbon whisky, and the Kentucky Derby.

Kentucky's most beloved agrarian symbol, a bluegrass tobacco barn, keeps vigil
under an overcast, winter morning sky. Old Frankfort Pike, Woodford County.

Above: A Spencer County fence, symbolizing the casualness of much of Kentucky's countryside, wanders between pond and meadow. *Right:* Historic Floyd's Fork glides from beneath a wooded bower on a chilly November morning in Jefferson County. The stream was a settler's route up from the Ohio.

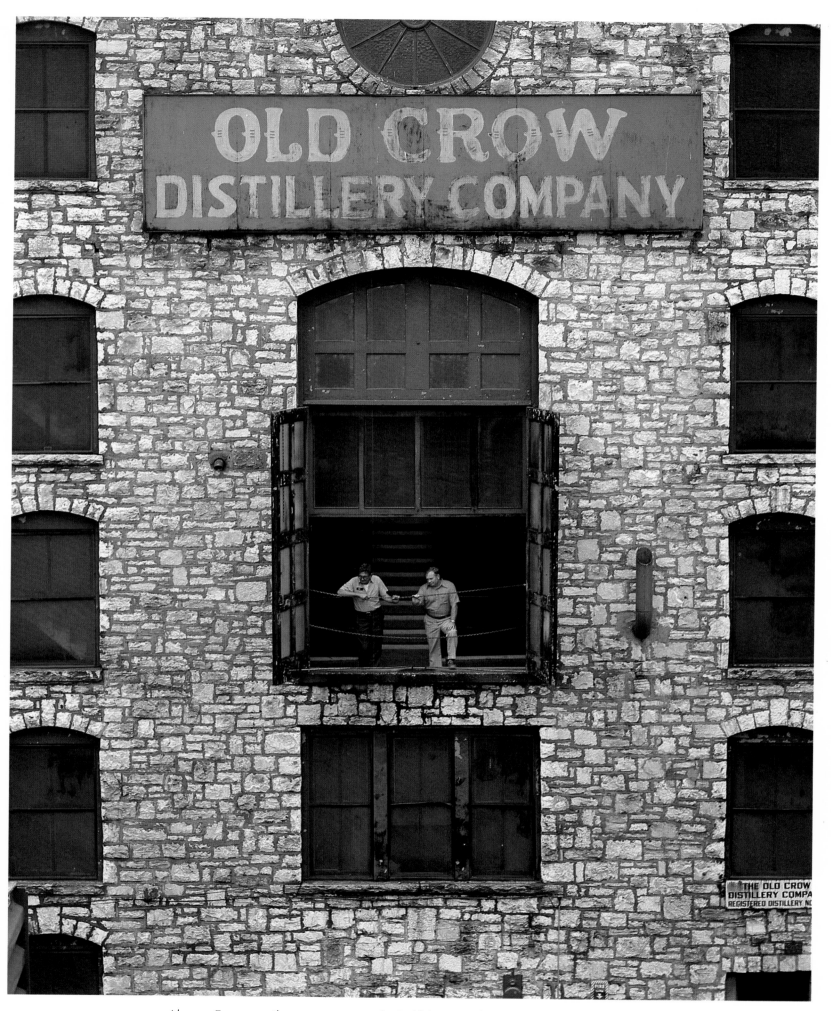

Above: For more than a century and a half the portals of the Old Crow Distillery on the Kentucky River at Millville, Woodford County, have released a generous flow of bourbon whisky. *Left:* Autumn's final, intoxicated fling in the Bernheim Forest, a privately maintained preserve in Bullitt County.

A Center Family House bedroom at Pleasant Hill, Mercer County. Dressed in Shaker garb, a hostess of this restored socio-religious, celibate community sits amid characteristic hand-crafted furniture.

Above: Drivers and horses near the finish line of Lexington's Red Mile in the elimination trials of the Annual Kentucky Futurity. *Overleaf:* Thoroughbred yearlings gallop through freshly fallen snow on the Airdrie Farm near Midway on the Old Frankfort Pike.

Childhood, a lazy summer day, and time to dream. Slick Ford, Wayne County, near the Tennessee border.

Above: Ravens Run in Fayette County has spent millions of years gnawing its way through a thick limestone slab on its journey to the Kentucky River. Here it flows placidly at the beginning of spring. *Overleaf:* Thoroughbreds graze before one of Calumet Farm's stud barns. From this setting come some of horse racing's most distinguished stakes winners.

Tobacco, a thirteen-month crop, involves entire farm families. In the cutting season, the ripe burley stalks are handled assembly-line fashion. Here, sticks of tobacco are handed up to the highest tier rails in an air-curing barn.

Towering super-structure of the Clay's Ferry Bridge just above famous Bull's Hell on a characteristically foggy morning. Spanning the Kentucky River, the bridge forms a slender link between North and South on crowded Highway I-75.

Above: The dome of the Kentucky State Capitol towers above the autumn foliage of tree-lined Capitol Avenue in Frankfort. *Right:* Reminiscent of an age when riverboats dominated the Ohio River, the *Belle of Louisville* paddles homeward, its wheel turning up a "brush pile" of water.

Above: Gracious, early twentieth century suburban homes line Louisville's Cherokee Parkway just outside famous Cherokee Park: *Left:* An old Jefferson County gristmill buried deep in a sylvan dell. Its worn wheel and stones have turned grain into meal and flour for almost two centuries.

Two-time, five-gaited, world champion, Imperator goes through a morning workout with his trainer in Shelby County. From the stables of standard-bred farms come an annual crop of harness and saddle horses competing on world-wide circuits.

Winter's chill traps early morning fog in a silver gossamer beneath the Palisades on the Kentucky River. Near the Brooklyn Bridge in Jessamine County, currents of wind and temperature create chilled spectres.

Inside the famous new world basilica of the gothic Cathedral of the Assumption in Covington. The Cathedral is a testimony to man's reverence for God and to the art of one of the main elements of Kentucky's immigrant population.

Above: This four-arched limestone bridge above the Glass Mill pool on Indian Creek has withstood time and traffic to become an honored monument. *Overleaf:* A broad field of Kentucky fescue spreads a soft, natural carpet before a Kentucky tobacco barn on a snowless winter day.

The earliest settlers brought country music west. Here, fiddlers and guitarists accompany folk singers in the Old Time Fiddlers Convention at Rough River State Park, Grayson County. These annual affairs perpetuate Kentucky's tradition as a conservator of its musical past.

Above: Ardent Kentucky basketball fans jam the Rupp Arena in Lexington's Civic Center where University of Kentucky teams have long enjoyed national success.
Overleaf: Viewed from the Indiana shore, Louisville casts dazzling streamers across the great basin just above the historic Falls of the Ohio.

Historic Federal Hill, in My Old Kentucky Home State Park, Bardstown, is tucked away behind a golden screen of autumn foliage. Receiving a constant stream of visitors throughout the year, it represents many of the state's romantic traditions.

Evening descends on the midway, Kentucky State Fairgrounds, Louisville. Here the worlds of Kentucky rural farm folk and commercial entertainers merge in a brilliant late-summer festival of color and excitement.

Long a cultural center, Louisville's Civic Orchestra, Ballet Company, and theatrical groups enjoy region-wide popularity. Here in the McCauley Theater, members of the Louisville Ballet Company perform a scene from *The Trojan Women*.

More than three thousand runners fill Lexington's Main Street at the start of the annual 10,000-meter foot race. Young and old test their wind, stamina, and courage against a circuitous course.

The moment of truth in Derby Week's great Balloon Race. Spectators surge around the colorful assembly of entries on the Kentucky State Fairgrounds in Louisville. Where the balloons go, where they land, is a matter of skill and fate.

Sunrise, reflected on the surface of fog-enshrouded Lake Cumberland and its surrounding hills in Russell County. This man-created impoundment is popular with fishermen, boaters, and other water sportsmen.

Paint Lick Creek in Garrard County tumbles beneath its foggy trail between knobby ridges to join the Kentucky River. The Creek's valley spreads across part of the western face of the knob country and bluegrass frontier.

Ashland, home of Henry Clay, Speaker of the United States House of Representatives, Senator, Secretary of State, and compromiser, is blanketed by deep winter snow. Icy branches of an old tulip poplar, bronze beech, and Scotch pine, which Clay is said to have planted on the spacious grounds, bend under their weight.

Morning tea on a chaste Greek Revival porch in stately Danville exemplifies the social tempo of life in old-settled, central Kentucky towns. This way of life is a link to a cherished past and an adamant barrier against radical change in the future. The homes remain ramparts of Kentucky graciousness.

Above: Kentucky thoroughbreds continue to sell for record prices at the Selected Yearling Sales at Keeneland. Annually, young racing prospects are sold under the auctioneer's hammer. *Overleaf:* The Rockcastle River's rock-strewn bed, which defied pioneer travelers in 1775, lies buried under forest cover.

A moment of intense concentration as rider and mount complete a jump at the Kentucky Horse Park near Lexington. Man and beast push to the limits of endurance in the Park, which hosts equestrian events, including Olympic trials.

Above: Since the 1800s the tiny country store at Rabbit Hash, on the Ohio River in Boone County, has withstood floods and hard times. *Overleaf:* Waning summer ritual: a sun-tanned youth works in a sea of golden burley leaves on the Pin Oak Farm, Woodford County.

The classical marble temple just above Sinking Spring in LaRue County shelters the humble log cabin said to be the home of Tom and Nancy Hanks Lincoln and the birthplace of their son, Abraham. The structure symbolizes the rise of a poor backwoods boy who became a man of the ages.

A field of Kentucky Derby horses rounds the first quarter pole. In the background are the twin towers of Churchill and throngs of race enthusiasts crowded into the stands and infield. In a matter of moments, a new name will join the list of more than one hundred Derby winners.

From time immemorial sand-bar willows have pushed up their spindly stems in flood and drouth to line the Ohio and Mississippi rivers. Here they anticipate spring and the rising and falling of the Ohio near Smithland in Ohio County.

WESTERN KENTUCKY

Gently rolling agrarian hills give way to western lowlands, where luxurious riverboats ply the Mississippi, and lazy cypress swamps, deafeningly silent in the summer heat, are reminders of Kentucky's lasting kinship with life in the Deep South.

An Ohio County farmstead viewed across the placid surface of a fish pond on a brilliant evening. Economically and spiritually, this farm and thousands like it document the Kentucky dream of agrarian well-being. The land has ever been a foundation and source of security for the state's rural people.

Above: Sailboats becalmed in the Kentucky Dam Village State Park Marina. Long corridors of man-made lakes have made sailing popular. *Right:* A great blue heron poised above its nest in the Higginson-Henry Wild Life Area, Union County. Every April these graceful birds return to their age-old rookery.

Above: A lazy autumn river setting in western Kentucky, leaves floating away and returning to the soil. *Left:* Nothing hinders spring fishing. These women cast for bass and crappie amid cypress trees on Big Turner Lake in Ballard County.

The towering obelisk in Fairview marks the birthplace of Jefferson Davis, President of the Confederacy. Eventually the Davis family left Todd County and took the emigrant road south to the cotton lands of Mississippi.

Above: Shedding the pall of winter, the brilliant redbud, or Judas tree, heralds the approach of spring in a pasture near Greenville, Muhlenberg County. *Overleaf:* On the surface of a primitive iron-rich lake in the Land Between the Lakes, American lotus in regal summer glory grow profusely.

Kentuckians always have relied on corn as a mainstay of food and liquid refresh-
ment. A Calloway County farmer anticipates the approach of winter by the old
method of shocking green fodder.

Above: Coal barges filled with "black gold" pass through the Tennessee Valley Authority's Kentucky Dam at the lower end of Kentucky Lake on the Tennessee River. *Overleaf:* The gently rolling Pennyrile farm landscape near Bowling Green in Warren County contrasts sharply with the hillside patch-fields of Appalachia.

The subtle images of early morning reflect on the mirror-like surface of Murphy's Pond in Hickman County, created by the great New Madrid Earthquake of 1811. Among the aquatic residents of its five hundred acres is a plentiful crop of cottonmouth moccasins.

The arching bridge which spans Lake Barkley near Aurora conveys traffic into the Land Between the Lakes, a 170,000-acre Tennessee Valley Authority reservation. Extending northward from Dover, Tennessee into Kentucky, the reservation serves as a natural retreat for all the Middle West.

Above: White-tail deer in a winter grazing ground have reclaimed their rightful domain in Kentucky's fabulous Land Between the Lakes. *Right:* The wind-blown Mississippi River is choppy as it flows in golden sunlight beneath the high bluffs of the famous Confederate fortification at Columbus, in Hickman County.

Above: In Fulton County along Kentucky's southwestern corner, a young cypress brake pushes slender boles up from the bottomless muck of a Mississippi River slough. *Left:* Blue phlox bloom in the Pennyrile State Park, Christian County.

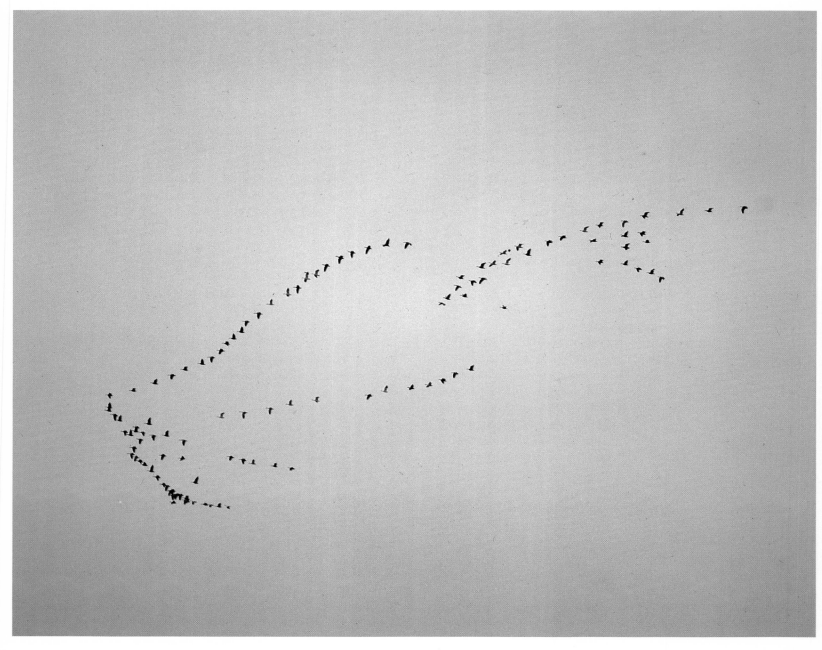

Above: A flock of giant Canadian geese migrate down the Mississippi fly-way to winter with thousands of their kind. *Right:* Three mist-shrouded cypress keep watch over a frozen pond in the Peal Land Wildlife Area bordering the Ohio River in Ballard County.

Above: Mallards rise from a cypress pond in the Reelfoot Wildlife Refuge. *Left:* The sternwheeler *Delta Queen,* a scheduled, passenger-carrying boat, paddles its way upstream on the Ohio near Owensboro. *Overleaf:* A towboat and its string of barges await passsage through Kentucky Dam locks on the Tennessee River.

At Sunset, the snags on Mitchell Lake in the Ballard County Wildlife Management Area stand as silent monuments to the changes in Kentucky's land since 1930, when the process of creating man-made lakes began.

Above: Early dawn behind the leafy screen of a leaning black willow on Lake Barkley near the Lake Barkley State Resort Park, Trigg County. *Overleaf:* A subtle summer glow highlights the broad expanse of Kentucky Lake backed up behind one of the great central river dams.

Above: American wild lotus leaves awash with morning dew in the Land Between the Lakes. The leaf blades measure twelve to twenty inches in diameter. *Right:* A lazy autumn day on the brush-lined Tradewater River in Christian County. Here, time itself seems to hang in suspension.

AFTERWORD

On the first Saturday in May, Kentucky opens its window and invites us to join in the exuberant celebration of its most honored tradition, the Kentucky Derby. I first looked through that window some twenty-five years ago, far from Louisville, at my parents' home in Western Pennsylvania. From that moment I have felt a sense of closeness to Kentucky and its people.

I passed through Kentucky for the first time in 1963. My friend Bob O'Laughlin and I fought our way through the eastern mountains over the incredibly twisting convulsions of old U.S. 119. On a cold and rainy late winter day, my '59 Chevy struggled up the side of one mountain and down the next. We inched our way through the narrow streets of the coal towns of Harlan, Whitesburg, and Pikeville, and through a hundred lesser known places like Partridge, Payne Gap, and Zebulon. It took us nearly five hours to cross less than one hundred and fifty miles of the most rugged and remote country I had ever seen. In spite of the mud-streaked windshield, slow-moving trucks and dangerous curves, I could not deny that this was a place of profound beauty. I realized then that there was more to the Bluegrass State than a two-minute horse race on a warm Saturday in May. Six years later I moved to Kentucky and I have made it my home ever since.

Kentucky is a magnificent place to photograph. It possesses an abundance of subtle landscapes and more than enough natural and historical phenomena to fill several photographic volumes. The ancient hills of Eastern Kentucky rise from the earth like blunted spires, harboring a rare botanical and geological collection unequaled in the Northern Hemisphere. Central Kentucky is dominated by the fertile, limestone-based bluegrass plateau, world-famous home to hundreds of elegantly manicured horse farms and a deeply rooted cultural and historic tradition dating back to the American colonial period. Finally, the gently rolling farms of Western Kentucky give way to fertile waterways and wildlife sanctuaries and to the cypress swamps of the Mississippi River lowlands. It was a joy for me to travel and record this diverse and wondrous state.

The first photograph for this book was taken in October, 1979. Ironically, it was the image selected to appear on the cover. The last photograph was taken inside Mammoth Cave in October, 1981. During those two years I drove more than sixty-five thousand miles, walked almost three hundred, and recorded thousands of images.

I wish it were possible to list everyone who helped and encouraged me during the creation of this book. There are hundreds of Kentuckians whose time and energy directly contributed to many of the photographs presented here.

I could not, however, close this book without acknowledging the following persons whose enduring faith and support I will value always: Anthea Boarman, Frank Clearfield, Peggy Cox, Brenda Thomlinson and Vickie Wilmes.

Lastly and most importantly, to my family, my parents John and June and my sister Kathy, for their love, support and encouragement, I will be forever grateful.

James Archambeault
Lexington, Kentucky